# SIMPLE PLAY
## easy fun for babies

by Rachel Coley, MS, OT/L

Published by CanDo Kiddo, LLC

**"For children, play is serious learning."** -Mr. Rogers

**"Play is the highest form of research."** -Albert Einstein

**"Play is the work of the child."** -Maria Montessori

Research shows that play is critical for early childhood development, but what many parents don't realize is that playing with a baby doesn't have to be complicated. Many of the simplest activities and toys (or household objects) are the most developmentally valuable. In this book, you'll see that you don't have to fill your home with expensive "educational" toys and programming to give your little one an enriched environment.

This book was written at the request of many parents who found my first book, *Begin With A Blanket: Creative Play for Infants*, helpful and who wanted activities for their "bigger babies." I hesitated at first because I felt that the activities I did with my own "bigger baby" were far from Pinterest or blog-worthy. They weren't flashy or exciting; they were ... SIMPLE. After some thought, I realized that's the point - and maybe that's what you need to hear: that playing with your baby doesn't have to be complicated.

In this book, I'll show you simple play activities to keep your baby busy and help build lifelong cognitive, sensory and motor skills.

Happy Playing!

Rachel

# ABOUT THE AUTHOR

Rachel Coley, MS, OT/L, is a licensed Occupational Therapist with over 10 years of experience working exclusively with children with 4 of those years specifically devoted to infants and toddlers. She has advanced specialized training in infant neurodevelopment, sensory processing, Torticollis and Plagiocephaly (infant neck and head shape issues). Rachel has participated in research and humanitarian projects related to the extreme deprivation of early movement and play in Romanian orphanages.

Rachel lives in Charlotte, North Carolina, with her husband, two kiddos and wonderdog. She enjoys mountain biking, whitewater kayaking and teaching and practicing yoga.

Learn more and keep in touch at CanDoKiddo.com and the CanDo Kiddo Facebook page.

# BONUS MATERIALS

In addition to the activities in this book, I'd like to share a collection of free bonus materials with you:

- Printable Onesie Stickers to photo-document your baby's age and developmental milestones

- A list of 50 Real Food First Meals for baby

- A printable First Foods Log

- A guide to the Top 10 most Frequently Asked Questions from CanDo Kiddo readers

To receive your bonus materials, simply visit

**www.candokiddo.com/bonus**

or scan the this QR code from your mobile device

# YOUR BABY'S TIMELINE

As babies get older, development begins to unfold at much more variable ranges. For that reason, this book won't designate ages for activities. Instead, I'll categorize activities into four motor stages:

Try activities for **Sitters**

- when your baby shows good head control in sitting when held
- when your baby shows the signs of sitting readiness described in the next section of this book

Try activities for **Crawlers**

- when your baby is on the move (including all forms of scooching, commando crawling, caterpillar wiggling and any other form of locomotion)

Try activities for **Standers**

- when your baby pulls to a stand
- when your baby comfortably bears weight through her feet

Try activities for **Cruisers**

- when your baby is stepping with support (from you or from furniture) and getting around on her feet for short distances
- when your baby is taking independent steps or walking

DON'T feel limited to using only the activities for the stage your baby is in. You can always keep using activities from previous stages with your kiddo.

# DISCLAIMER

Having a baby means being vigilant. All activities in this book are designed for close supervision. That means an adult within arms reach with eyes on baby.

Some activities include household or non-toy items that could be ingested or become strangulation hazards. Please use your own judgement with your child. Again, CLOSE supervision is required to keep baby safe. CanDo Kiddo, LLC, is not liable for any injury incurred while replicating any activity found within this book.

Rachel Coley is a licensed Occupational Therapist. Any advice in this book is not a replacement for medical advice from a physician. Please consult your child's pediatrician if you suspect any medical or developmental issues with your child. These tips do not replace the relationship between therapist and client in a one-on-one treatment session with an individualized treatment plan based on a professional evaluation.

# SIMPLE PLAY FOR Sitters

# IS MY BABY READY TO SIT?

Propping a floppy baby in sitting before she's ready isn't good for spinal development or sensory development and can be counter-productive to your child learning how to sit. Products marketed as baby seats, such as the popular Bumbo, are best used once your baby shows readiness for sitting and not before.

## How will you know your baby is ready to sit? Here are 3 signs to look for:

1. when you hold your little one and she sits nice and tall with her head held steady and without rounding her back

2. when she's beginning to put hands out to try to stop a fall when placed in sitting with very close supervision

3/ when she's working on getting into a hands-and-knees position when placed on her belly.

Once you see those signs, the best sitting practice is on a firm, padded surface with plenty of room to wobble and self-correct. Too much support from baby seats keeps your baby upright but doesn't allow her the opportunity to sense and respond to her weight shifting in order to stay upright on her own. Instead, use use soft props to help keep your little one safe while she practices sitting on a firm surface.

The best sitting practice for baby before you see those signs of readiness is when she's supported by adult hands. This allows you to offer support that responds to baby's body and efforts. An attentive caregiver automatically helps baby come back to center when she leans off-kilter. A baby seat allows baby to slump and lean without any cues or assistance to maintain upright.

# SUPPORTING A WOBBLY SITTER

Once baby shows signs of readiness for sitting, try these tricks to keep baby safe from the inevitable tumbles of the first weeks of practicing (with close supervision, of course):

Use a soft crescent-shaped nursing pillow, like a Boppy, behind baby to help protect from falls to the back or sides.

Place baby (with supervision) in a small basket, storage container or diaper box that comes up at least to her armpits or shoulders.

Use interlocking foam floor mats (that often have alphabet letters on them) to create a corner chair against a wall or cabinet.

Use a baby bathtub (without water, of course) to give baby a little extra support.

Place baby in sitting with her back to the corner of a Pack 'n Play or similar play yard.

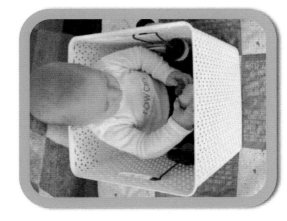

# A SLEIGH RIDE

Just because your little one isn't crawling yet doesn't mean he can't enjoy the sensation of moving through your home. Once your baby is a steady sitter, you can use things you have in your house to make a "sleigh" and pull your little one on a ride.

We had a an empty box and a very steady sitter, but a laundry basket would offer higher sides if your little one is still wobbly. If you don't have rope, a dog leash or belt will do for a handle. Just be sure to safely store these items out of reach when the activity is done.

Not only is this a fun way to add movement to your child's day, it requires baby to process sensory inputs from the world around him and from his own body in order to maintain his balance in a moving sleigh. Play that requires your child to formulate a skilled or purposeful response (staying upright, in this case) to sensory inputs is the real heart of "sensory play!"

BENEFITS: balance, movement sense, vision, pressure & stretch sense, core strength

See the Glossary of Terms at the end of this book for technical terminology of benefits listed.

# BALL PLAY

Your kiddo is months away from throwing or catching a ball, but babies are fascinated by these shiny round objects and eager to reach, touch, hold and drool all over them. Each of your baby's arms is controlled by a different half of her brain. Activities that encourage her to hold and manipulate objects with both hands stimulate the coordination of both sides of her brain.

No need to buy a fancy ball that sings the alphabet or creates a light show when touched. Babies are learning even from the simple sensations of a smooth playground ball or bumpy sensory ball. The cause and effect of watching a ball roll and bounce when dropped is sufficient to capture most babies' attention and is promoting learning.

If you have an older sibling or other adult handy, roll a ball back and forth and let your baby watch. Or have one adult sit behind baby to help trap a ball rolled to her. Watching a rolling ball is great for visual development.

BENEFITS: sense of touch, pressure & stretch sense, vision, eye movement skills, attention, using two hands together, upper body strength, core strength, balance, hand-eye coordination

# SEATED WATER PLAY

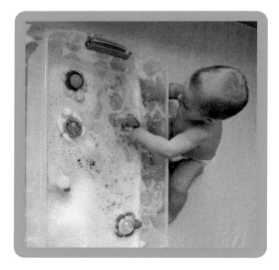

Babies love water play so why reserve it for bathtime? Add water, bubbles and bath toys to a large, shallow storage container and prepare for your baby (and the area around the container) to get soaked.

See that nifty twisting maneuver in the photo on the right? This marks a huge developmental milestone most parents don't know about. This rotation of the body over one hip and thigh is a transitional movement that will help your baby navigate into and out of sitting and hands-and-knees on his own. It's one of several movements that are critical for baby learning to crawl on hands and knees. Activities that encourage reaching across the body in sitting help promote this rotation. It's also important to not always immediately retrieve toys that roll (or float) out of reach. Sometimes that's just the motivation your little one needs to try a new skill! Your baby will need to get nice and steady in sitting before he attempts rotation, so if you're not seeing it yet, don't worry. Just keep playing! And as always - CLOSE SUPERVISION is required for safety!

BENEFITS: sense of touch, body awareness, core strength, balance, grasping skills

# RUBBER BANDS ON A BOARD BOOK

Did you know that "book handling" is an important pre-reading skill? According to The National Center for Infants, Toddlers and Families*, important early literacy behaviors for babies include those "related to a child's physical manipulation or handling of books, such as page turning and chewing."

Most typically developing babies won't be able to turn pages of a board book until 9-12 months of age and won't turn single pages until 12-18 months. Want to make book handling and play more fun for your baby before that time? Wrap rubber bands around the spine of your book to separate a few of the pages. This will keep them from sticking together and help your little one to turn them before she can separate them on her own.

Be sure to take the rubber bands off after each reading time so that they don't damage the spine of the book.

**Caution** - rubber bands can snap and be swallowed. Using fabric hair elastics can reduce the risk but as with all CanDo Kiddo activities, close supervision (eyes on baby within arm's reach) is required.

BENEFITS: early literacy, vision, touch sense, hand-eye coordination, grasping, using hands together

*School Readiness: Birth to Three - Literacy. From:

http://main.zerotothree.org/site/PageServer?pagename=ter_par_012_literacy

# GLOW STICKS FUN

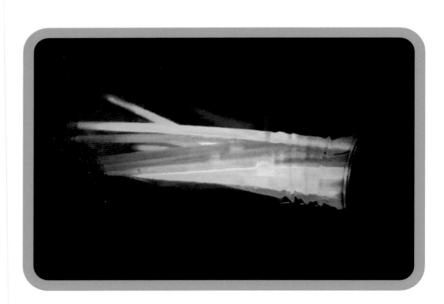

So many fun things are off limits to babies because they put everything in their mouths. But by using simple clear containers around your house, you can keep baby safe while letting him visually explore new and exciting sights - like glow sticks!

Simply place multi-colored glow sticks in a clear water bottle or plastic food storage container and let your baby play in a dark or dimly lit room. Your little one will enjoy shaking, dropping, rolling and drooling all over this new activity.

BENEFITS: vision, touch sense, grasping skills, using hands together, hand-eye coordination

# PLAYING AT THE REFRIGERATOR

Once your little one gets more steady in a sitting position, the possibilities for where you can sit her for play open up. The handles of your refrigerator make a great spot to hang toys for your baby to explore, shake, pull and play with.

Place a soft blanket on the floor in front of your fridge and use ribbon or plastic link toys to hang teether toys, stuffed toys, rattles and more from your refrigerator or freezer handles. The same concept can work hanging from cabinet or drawer handles as long as you use child-safe locks to secure doors and drawers.

It won't be long before your baby is fully mobile and won't stay in one spot, so enjoy the last weeks or months of quiet, seated play! As with all CanDo Kiddo activities, close supervision (eyes on baby within arm's reach) is required – hanging toys can pose a strangulation risk.

BENEFITS: sense of touch, vision, pressure & stretch sense, balance, using hands together, upper body strength, core strength, grasping skills, hand-eye coordination

# SWINGING AT THE PARK

Once your kiddo can sit with an upright spine and head held upright, you can place him in a playground bucket-style baby swing provided it has a barrier between the legs to keep your little one from sliding out. Most of these swings have very large seats, so bring a blanket along to the park to fold and place behind your baby to customize the fit of the seat for your little one.

Once your baby begins sitting, his whole orientation to the world will become upright. His natural instinct, based on sensory information from the movement and pressure & stretch senses, will be to hold his body and head up. He's ready to sit upright in a standard stroller (or in the child seat of a shopping cart) instead of a car seat travel system and to swing in a seated position instead of a reclined infant swing.

BENEFITS: movement sense, eye movement skills, socialization and bonding, core strength, balance,

# FLASHLIGHT PLAY

Flashlight play is fun for babies of all ages but now that your little one is sitting up, her hands are free to explore, shake, roll and bang glowing objects together. Make your own glowing toys by dropping small flashlights or LED keychain lights into colored food containers or water bottles. This keeps your little one from mouthing the flashlights and diffuses the light into soft colors. This is a great activity for cloudy or rainy day fun!

It's easy to think that the most educational toys are the ones that sing the ABC's or say words to our babies. Even simple toys and household objects offer rich learning opportunities and are often more responsive to your baby's actions. Remember that everything in this world is new for your baby and her innate drive is to explore and learn. Play doesn't have to be fancy to capture her interest and promote her development.

BENEFITS: vision, sense of touch, attention, using hands together, balance, grasping skills, hand-eye coordination

# SIMPLE PLAY FOR Crawlers

# ROLL A BALL DOWN THE SLIDE

Playgrounds are a great way to get outside with your baby, but it can be challenging to find activities for such a small kiddo at the park. One fun activity for your crawling baby is to roll a soft ball down a slide to your waiting baby at the bottom. This is a great activity to enlist the help of older kids or siblings.

Your baby will begin to anticipate the ball coming and will work on following the ball with his eyes as it moves down the slide. He likely won't be catching the ball yet, instead chasing it as it rolls past him. This game is great for promoting language skills - positional words like "up/down", "on top/at the bottom", and words like "ready, set, go" or "more".

BENEFITS: pressure & stretch sense, touch sense, vision, eye movement skills, attention, socialization and bonding, using hands together, core strength, balance, hand-eye coordination, speech

# BABY POOL WATER PLAY

A small baby pool (inflatable or hard plastic) makes a great spot for your crawling baby to enjoy water play and to practice crawling over obstacles as he navigates getting in and out. Water play stimulates your baby's senses of touch, vision and hearing as he hears the water splashing and pouring.

In warmer climates, a pool can be placed on a patio, porch, driveway or in the yard for a change of scenery. In colder climates, bring your pool inside and bump the heat up a few degrees for indoor water play. Lay several layers of towels around your pool and only fill it with enough water to splash to minimize messes.

Cups, pitchers, sieves and strainers make great household items for water play - in addition to bath toys and waterproof toys you have.

As you keep reading you'll see that a small baby pool makes a great toy purchase - it's versatile enough for all sorts of activities beyond water play!

As with all CanDo Kiddo activities, close, direct supervision is required. A baby can drown in very small amounts of water so never  turn  your attention away during water play, even for a moment.

# GOLF BALL PAINTING

Little ones won't know they're creating adorable art as they shake, bang and sling during this fun activity, but you'll be left with a baby-made masterpiece to keep or give as a gift to a loved one.

Tape paper to the bottom of a shallow lidded container, preferably with a clear lid. Add a golfball or two and some globs of non-toxic paint. Other small balls work fine but the weight and sound of bumpy golfballs make this activity extra fun! Close the container tightly and tape it if it's not 100% secure. Then hand the container off to your kiddo to make a work of art! She'll hear the balls rolling inside, feel the weight in the container shift and see the balls inside move as she plays.

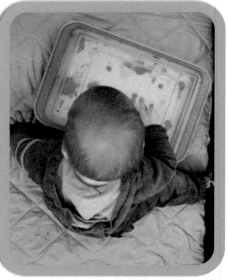

Once baby has had her fun (remember, it may only be a few minutes and that's perfectly normal and okay), open the container carefully and let the paint dry completely before trying to remove the paper. Paper still wet with paint tends to rip and tear when removed. You can leave the final product as is or cut out a shape to mount on a larger piece of paper or onto a card for a sweet memento created by little hands.

BENEFITS: pressure & stretch sense, hearing sense, vision, eye movement skills, attention, using hands together, upper body strength, grasping skills

# TUNNEL PLAY

A simple play tunnel is a great open-ended toy for your growing and learning baby. Open-ended toys promote exploration and discovery, can be used in a wide variety of ways to play, and tend to grow well with your child through multiple ages and stages. I recommend that families try to balance their child's "toy diet" with plenty of open ended toys. Here are just a few of the endless tunnel play activities for crawling babies:

**Giant Ball Ramp** : Using pillows, a piece of furniture, or a staircase to elevate one end of the tunnel, roll a soft ball down to your baby and let her crawl to chase those that roll past.

**Peek-a-boo** : With either baby or you in the tunnel, pull the top edge of one end of the tunnel down to the floor to close it off. Letting go gives a nice dramatic "Peek-a-Boo!"

**Shake, Shake!** : Sit at opposite ends of the tunnel and show your little one how to shake, shake! This can be especially fun if you put stuffed animals, balls or other toys in the tunnel to shake. Add in some language and direction-following play by saying, "STOP" and "GO" or letting your kiddo call the shots!

**Ball in the Hoop** : Use the velcro closures or ties to collapse your tunnel into a flat hoop. Let your baby or toddler drop balls through the hoop as you hold it.

**Over The Mountain** : Tunnel play can get more exciting when you add throw pillows, rolled blankets and other soft obstacles underneath the tunnel to crawl over.

**Commute** : Little kids love activities such as puzzles or ball/car ramps positioned at one end of the tunnel with the pieces at the opposite end. They'll have to commute back and forth through the tunnel to complete their task. This is awesome for developing sustained attention, and for learning to complete multi-step sequences

**Popcorn** : As your kiddo crawls through the tunnel, shake it until she giggles! Feel free to borrow this little rhyme as you play: "Popcorn on a string, let's see (your child's name) pop this thing. Pop pop pop, pop pop pop pa-pop! Pop pop pop, pop pop pa-pop! Pop pop pop, pop pop pa-pop! And now we STOP!" This makes a fun turn-taking group activity.

**Water play** : Most tunnels are made out of tent-like nylon material that will dry quickly without damage. If yours is, take your tunnel outside for water play - letting your kiddo crawl into a baby pool or crawl under a sprinkler through her tunnel.

Don't have a play tunnel? Some of these activities can be enjoyed with a large cardboard box with both ends open.

BENEFITS: pressure & stretch sense, sense of touch, movement sense, hearing sense, vision, body awareness, attention, socialization & bonding, upper body strength, leg strength, core strength, grasping, speech

# CARROT PEEL SENSORY PLAY

Food makes a great sensory play material - even when it's not mealtime. Learning to touch objects that are a wide variety of textures - wet, slimy, sticky, bumpy, scratchy, etc. - is an important part of sensory development. Through positive, playful interactions with textures, your baby learns that these new sensations are not threatening or uncomfortable.

Thoroughly wash and peel carrot or two, placing the peels in a shallow container or on a high chair tray. With close supervision (eyes on baby within arm's reach), let baby explore the cold, wet peels through touch. Do not let baby mouth or chew peels as a piece could break off and become a choking hazard.

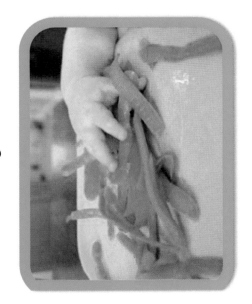

Sensory play with textures is great for picky eaters, for babies who don't like to open or bear weight through their hands in Tummy Time or crawling, and for babies who become distressed with grooming tasks like tooth brushing, face wiping and hair combing.

BENEFITS: sense of touch, sense of smell, using hands together, grasping skills

# DOWN A SLIDE ON BELLY

Believe it or not, once he can crawl your baby is old enough to start enjoying some playground equipment with your help and close supervision. A great skill for a crawling baby to learn is to turn around and back off of heights safely. How do you teach that?! Through play, of course!

Rather than placing your baby belly-down on the slide each time, allow her to crawl forward toward the slide with your hands right there or your hand holding one leg. Use a key phrase - "turn around," "feet first," etc. each time and offer as little help as possible for your little one to swing his feet around and ease down the slide on his belly, feet first.

This is a great way to encourage your baby's *motor planning* - or problem-solving with the body. By giving your little one the opportunity to try turning around for himself (with you right there for safety and for help if needed), you allow him to learn the valuable skill of figuring out new motor challenges. You also get to practice the valuable parenting skill of waiting and letting your little one work through problems.

If you live in a very hot climate, be sure to check the temperature of the slide surface before letting your little one go down. Live in a colder climate? Many kid-friendly restaurants and shopping malls have indoor playground equipment. Or you could always invest in a small indoor slide for your home (often available used at consignment stores).

BENEFITS: pressure & stretch sense, sense of touch, movement sense, body awareness

# PUZZLES

Puzzles for a baby? Long before your kiddo is even thinking about putting puzzle pieces in, she'll be able to take them out. Large-piece wooden puzzles are safe for mouthing babies and have knobs that make for great grasping practice for your little one.

Even one wooden puzzle can be tweaked to make for many puzzle discovery activities. Simply cut out photos of family members or cut pictures out of magazines of animals, food, etc. and tape them into the holes of a wooden puzzle. Your baby will love discovering what's hiding underneath those pieces!

BENEFITS: sense of touch, pressure & stretch sense, vision, attention, grasping skills, hand-eye coordination

# PILLOW CRAWL

Once your baby has figured out a way to be mobile - whether it's through crawling, creeping (belly on floor), commando crawling, rolling or scooting - you can challenge his strength and his movement problem-solving by having him crawl over pillows.

Make a baby obstacle course with couch pillows or throw pillows on the floor to climb over in order to get a favorite toy (or a favorite person or pet). You can combine a pillow crawl with your play tunnel (or cardboard box), baby pool (or large, shallow storage container), and soft pieces of furniture pushed close to make narrow passages and more!

Pillow crawling is one of many play activities referred to as "heavy work" by Occupational Therapists. Heavy work activities require the use of big muscles of the body (legs, arms, belly and back) against resistance. This type of play has been observed to help children improve their sensory processing in other sensory systems. Heavy work can be a great activity to include just before mealtimes if you have a picky eater, before or after potentially over-stimulating outings or social gatherings, or before grooming tasks if you have a child who is resistant to tooth or hair brushing, etc.

BENEFITS: pressure & stretch sense, sense of touch, movement sense, body awareness, upper body strength, leg strength, core strength, balance

# BALL POOL

Make your own "ball pool" by throwing balls of various shapes and sizes into a small baby pool, bathtub or large laundry basket, or storage container. You don't have to invest in a set of plastic ball pit balls; we have several playground-style balls from the drugstore that work great.

Moving in a "pool" of balls gives your baby lots of input to the pressure & stretch sense. Her skin perceives the texture of the balls, her eyes perceive the shape and colors of the balls and you might be surprised to know that her muscles and joints have tiny receptors that perceive pressure and stretch information. Sensory information from these receptors and the brain's refined processing of that sensory information is vital for your child learning to move her body in a coordinated way.

BENEFITS: pressure & stretch sense, sense of touch, body awareness, using hands together, core strength, balance, grasping skills

# MISCHIEF BASKETS

Many parents notice that once their babies are mobile, toys hold much less interest than objects around the house. In our home, the least baby-safe items usually have the biggest appeal! One way to capture your baby's (very developmentally normal and healthy) interest in exploring is to provide what I like to call "mischief baskets."

A mischief basket (Montessori educators call them Discovery Baskets) is simply a container of some sort (box, bin, basket, bag) that contains new, baby-safe things for your little one to explore. You can "hide" mischief baskets around your home and change their contents frequently to keep your little one curious. Here are some ideas for mischief basket contents:

-clean socks, hats and mittens/gloves

-tupperware lids of all shapes and sizes

-measuring cups and spoons

-empty food containers

-baby comb, brush, washcloth, toothbrush

-whisks, spatulas, and large serving utensils

-clean, empty plastic containers

-disposable straws

-clean spice containers filled with fresh herbs, cinnamon sticks, lemon slices, orange peels, etc.

-opaque containers filled (and taped shut) with various dried goods such as rice, beans, spoons, etc. to make different sounds

BENEFITS: sense of touch, vision, hearing sense, sense of smell, pressure & stretch sense, attention, using hands together, grasping skills, hand-eye coordination skills

# SIMPLE PLAY FOR Standers

# ICE BLOCK EXPLORATION

To make your ice block, place several water-proof toys or baby-safe objects in a medium to large food storage container. Add an inch of water and place in the freezer for several hours. Remove the toy-laden ice block from the container and place it on a shallow tray or baking sheet.

This is a fun sensory play activity, but unless you have an older sibling who can "excavate" the ice with a water dropper, sponge or toothbrush it will likely be an activity that you have to revisit for brief periods of play every 10 minutes or so as the ice melts.

Your little one will feel COLD on her hands and feel the sensation of toys poking out of the ice. As the ice melts, she can splash the water in the pan and try pulling her toys out of the slush.

BENEFITS: sense of touch, vision, using hands together, hand strength, grasping skills, hand-eye coordination

# HULA HOOPS

You may not have thought of hula hoops for baby play before. Just like play tunnels, hula hoops are an awesome open-ended toy that will grow with your child for years to come. So how would a baby play with a hula hoop?

Left to her own devices, your little one will likely use both hands to pick up the hula hoop. Using two hands together is a valuable skill for brain development and for motor coordination. She may shake the hoop(s), lift them up and drop them down. But with a little help from you, she can crawl through a hoop held upright or drop a ball in a hoop held flat above the floor. She can chase a hoop that's been rolled across the floor. She can imitate putting a hoop over her head or over a toy. You can use plastic toy links to make small circles around the hoop to shake and move. Tie short ribbons to the hula hoop to make streamers that wave when baby shakes the hoop.

BENEFITS: using hands together, grasping skills, hand-eye coordination, hand strength, core strength, balance, pressure & stretch sense, sense of touch, vision, eye movement skills, body awareness, attention, socialization & bonding.

# EXERCISE BALL STANDING

This is a fun way to play that helps your kiddo develop the balance it will take to transition from standing to walking. Either outside or in a room with no hard furniture within a "fall zone," stand baby up at a large exercise ball. You can show him how to bang it and how to roll it slightly forward and back or side to side. You can also sing a song or read a book with him as he stands.

Unlike a coffee table or the edge of a couch, an exercise ball provides your baby with lots of practice for dynamic standing balance - meaning balancing while moving. Because an exercise ball can move, it challenges you baby's sensory systems to perceive and respond to small changes - excellent for developing the movement and pressure & stretch senses essential for balanced walking.

Don't have an exercise ball? A rocking chair, porch swing, glider ottoman, or your legs can also provide dynamic support. If the object is hard, just be very vigilant to prevent injury.

BENEFITS: balance, body awareness, leg strength, core strength, pressure & stretch sense, movement sense, vision, socialization & bonding

# GIANT DRUMS

Most babies love to make noise and love music! Turn over a few large plastic containers (laundry baskets and large plastic storage bins work great) and place them close together on the floor. Turn on music and encourage your little one to stand at and drum his giant drums!

By having more than one drum, you encourage your baby to take small side-steps while still holding on. This is the beginning of "cruising," when your baby walks while holding onto furniture, walls and other objects.

Add language play into the activity by drumming "loud" and "soft" with your baby. Make it a freeze game by pausing the music and showing your baby how you "stop" drumming until the music starts again.

BENEFITS: balance, hearing sense, touch sense, pressure & stretch sense, socialization & bonding, speech

# PLAY WITH POUCHES

As your baby grows and learns, she's discovering that sometimes you can only see a small part of something that's actually much bigger. This is one of several important visual perceptual skills that she'll rely on often later in life when reading or trying to find a pencil in a cluttered desk, for example. One way to tap into your baby's expanding ability to explore things that she only sees part of is to partially hide toys inside of pouches.

Many things in your home can function as pouches - clean socks, soft-sided lunch bags, small wallets (completely emptied; make sure no change is left inside!), zippered cosmetic cases and travel toiletries bags, etc. Gather a few pouches and partially hide toys in them for your baby to discover and pull out. Pulling toys out of pouches also requires two hands - a lifelong skill called bilateral coordination.

BENEFITS: vision, attention, using hands together, grasping skills, pressure & stretch sense

# A MAGNET BOARD

A cookie sheet makes a perfect spot for refrigerator magnets for grasping play. Place the cookie sheet on a coffee table, low shelf or ottoman for your baby to play while standing or to pull onto the floor for seated exploration, like my kiddo did!

Magnet play is great for promoting grasping skills and hand strength. Typically around the time that babies get vertical - standing and cruising - they experience rapid development of their grasping abilities.

**Be sure** to only include magnets bigger than baby's fist to prevent choking.

BENEFITS: grasping, hand strength, hand-eye coordination, using hands together, vision, sense of touch, pressure & stretch sense

# DIY BALL RAMP

Ball ramps are great fun for little ones, but you can make one nearly anywhere with a few household materials. Use a cardboard poster tube, a clean piece of PVC pipe or simply roll a piece of cardboard and tape it into a tube shape. Elevate one end of the tube to make a ramp. Give your child a container of small (but not chokable) toys to put in the tube. It's okay if not all the toys fit – that makes for fun observations chock-full of language like "noooooo, it's too big!" and "yes, that one fits!"

Your child may need help orienting some objects or placing them gently in the tube. That's normal and okay. Some of the objects may not be round and may need you and your child to lift one end of the tube higher to slide them down. Part of the fun of these activities is joining in your child's play and discovering new ways to play!

BENEFITS: hand-eye coordination, grasping skills, speech, socialization & bonding, attention, vision, eye movement skills, hearing sense, sense of touch

# BABY"S CABINET OR DRAWER

Babies love imitating the adults in their lives. Imitation provides a wonderful avenue for learning. Your little one sees you open drawers and cabinets every time you're in the kitchen, so it's no wonder she's eager to do the same. In the midst of baby-proofing your home, find a cabinet or low drawer that you can leave unlocked. Keep some of baby's toys, books, or baby-safe household items inside. A great place to do this is in the kitchen - have a cupboard or drawer filled with empty, clean food containers or baby-safe kitchen utensils so that she can imitate what she sees you do during meal preparation and clean-up.

One of the many benefits of this type of play is the dynamic balance baby has to develop and maintain in order to open a cabinet or drawer while standing. She's learning to combine activating some muscles to give her stability while activating others to give movement.

All furniture should be anchored to the wall. **Do not let baby play in or near a piece of unanchored furniture.**

BENEFITS: balance, body awareness, pressure & stretch sense, grasping skills, hand-eye coordination, using hands together, socialization & bonding, sense of touch

# MESSY GOOP PLAY

Letting your baby experience a wide variety of textures in play is an excellent way to help him develop his sense of touch. One of my favorite places for messy play is an empty bathtub. Strip baby down to his diaper and let him get as messy as he wants knowing that clean-up will be a breeze. A baby pool also makes a great easy-to-clean spot.

Here's a simple recipe for baby-safe scented sensory goop:

2 cups cornstarch
1 cup water
1/4 to 1/2 packet Jello powder for color and scent

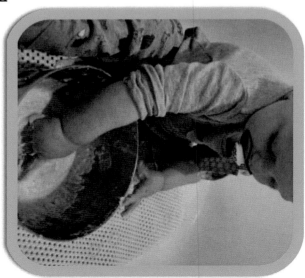

Parents often describe their babies and toddlers being resistant to touch or taste certain textures of food - often slimy, sticky, wet foods. Increasing your baby's opportunities for messy play is often an effective strategy for getting your little one less defensive around new sensations. Play is less threatening than mealtime and through positive, pleasant touch experiences, your baby learns that new sensations aren't scary. Try hiding waterproof toys in your goop to let your baby get messy finding them - giving a fun purpose to touching the mess.

BENEFITS: sense of touch, sense of smell, vision, attention, using hands together

# SIMPLE PLAY FOR Cruisers

# WHAT IS CRUISING?

Cruising is an intermediate skill most babies exhibit between standing and walking. It involves moving by stepping the feet while holding on to objects (typically furniture) with the hands.

Unlike standing, cruising requires your baby to shift her weight fully off of one foot in order to move it - a impressive new display of dynamic balance! It also requires her to navigate around objects and plan her next move in order to reach her goal.

# CUPS ON A COFFEE TABLE

Scatter baby-safe cups around a coffee table or across a low bench and watch your baby have a blast cruising to explore them. Toy stacking cups will work just fine but as I mentioned before, newly mobile babies typically bypass official "toys" in favor of household items every chance they can get.

Expand this activity by turning cups over and hiding toys or objects underneath. Show your baby how to talk or make animal noises into cups. Stack cups in a tower on the floor and let her pull to a stand and cruise to get more cups to add. Try different cups on your head as hats and make a silly face when they fall off. Through play, you'll naturally be repeating words like "more," "uh-oh," "on top", "that one," etc. - promoting language and social skills.

BENEFITS: balance, body awareness, grasping skills, hand-eye coordination, socialization & bonding, speech, attention, sense of touch, pressure & stretch sense, vision, hearing sense

# BABY "I SPY"

When it comes to language development, babies grow an extensive vocabulary of receptive language - what they understand - before their mouths can match it with their expressive language - what they say. You can capitalize on this with short games of 'I Spy', baby edition, throughout the day.

In each area of your home that baby frequents, select a few objects to be the subject of your 'I Spy' game. Initially, you'll tell baby, "I see a light," as you point to the light or "I see the apples" as you point to the basket of apples on your counter. After a few days of repeating the same few objects this way, pause after you tell baby what you see and wait to see if he looks toward the object. If so, recognize that baby sees the object and describe it a bit more, "You see the light, too! It's up high," or, "Yes, apples are on the counter. They are red!" If your baby doesn't yet look to the objects, continue pointing to them. Change up the few objects once your baby has mastered them to keep the game interesting and to help your kiddo learn new words.

Don't be surprised if pretty quickly you see your baby start to point to the objects you name throughout the day or point to other objects for you to name and talk about.

This game is excellent for language development and for baby's understanding of non-verbal communication cues like pointing and following someone's eye gaze to see what they're talking about.

BENEFITS: speech, socialization & bonding

# TAPE TOYS TO THE WALL

Once your baby is cruising, you may notice a newfound interest in all sorts of objects that were only a few weeks ago out of his reach! Channel your baby's curiosity into play by taping lightweight toys (we love using greeting cards and photos as well) to a wall or piece of furniture above baby's eye level but within arm's reach. A crib's railings can work nicely for this activity, and blue painter's tape or masking tape can help protect your home.

Reaching overhead is great for baby's shoulder strength. Shoulder strength is essential for his fine motor development. In order to make careful, coordinated movements with the hands and fingers, your child first needs good strength and stability in his core (belly and back), shoulder and arm muscles. You and I likely reach overhead dozens of times a day. Your baby has only been sitting and standing upright for a few months, so reaching his arms overhead against gravity is a new challenge.

BENEFITS: upper body strength, core strength, balance, body awareness, grasping skills, hand-eye coordination skills, vision, sense of touch, pressure & stretch sense

# HANGING BALL

Once your little one is standing with support, she'll have a blast playing with a suspended ball. Simply tape or tie a ribbon or thin rope to a large soft ball and hang it - from a countertop, a door frame or a tall piece of furniture. Remember that your little one will do best with the support of a firm object to hold on to, but look for a location without hard corners, sharp cabinet handles or other dangers in the likely event of a fall.

Visually following a moving target like a ball and timing a response to hit it is great for your child's motor planning and coordination. As your little one transitions into a walker, she'll have to make many timed responses to moving objects in her environment - especially other kids!

BENEFITS: balance, body awareness, eye movement skills, hand-eye coordination, vision, pressure & stretch sense, sense of touch, movement sense, attention, upper body strength, core strength

# LIDS IN A SLOT

Typically, around the time that kiddos are beginning to cruise and experiment with walking, they also have a growing interest in putting items into containers and taking them out again. You can make your own very simple first shape sorter for your baby by cutting a large slot in a big plastic container. Use masking, duct or packing tape to cover any sharp edges where you've made your cuts. Give your baby a stack of lids of various shape and sizes (larger than her fist) to place in the slot.

Your baby may need help orienting the lids to go in the slot but try to sit on your hands a bit and let her work through some trial and error. You may be surprised just how long your little one will work to figure out the new challenge. If your baby gets frustrated or looks at or calls out to you, join in and help her in her efforts.

Dumping things out of containers is also great fun at this age and may be your little one's favorite part of this activity!

BENEFITS: vision, hand-eye coordination, grasping skills, socialization & bonding, attention, sense of touch

# PUSH TOYS

Push toys allow your cruising baby to enjoy new freedoms - walking away from the furniture. He'll have to adjust his speed and body position to remain upright and he'll learn, over time, to steer to navigate around obstacles.

Sometimes it can be helpful to add some weight to your child's push toy to slow it down and keep it from toppling over. A 5 llb. bag of sugar or several 1 lb. bags of rice make great weights for this purpose.

Don't feel limited to store-bought toys. Wheeled storage bins or carts or a sturdy stroller can offer your baby great pushing fun, too.

BENEFITS: balance, body awareness, pressure & stretch sense, vision, movement sense, attention, core strength, leg strength

# BABY-SAFE PLAY DOUGH

Never thought to use play dough with babies this young? With taste-safe play dough and VERY close supervision, your little one can enjoy the sensations of squishing and squeezing, pushing, pulling and pinching - all great for fine motor strength and coordination. This is another great touch activity that can help your baby playfully enjoy new textures and sensations. He'll learn to process sticky or squishy textures as enjoyable and not threatening.

Here's a simple recipe for taste-safe play dough for babies:
Mix 1 cup baby rice cereal with 1 cup corn starch. Add 1/2 cup water, 3 tbsp coconut oil and 1/4 to 1/2 pack Jello powder for color and scent. Mix well with your hands and add very small amounts of water or corn starch to adjust consistency.

Your dough will last several days in a Ziplock baggie in the refrigerator.

BENEFITS: sense of touch, sense of smell, pressure & stretch sense, hand strength, vision, hand-eye coordination, using hands together, attention, grasping skills

# GLOSSARY OF KEY TERMS

Pressure & Stretch Sense : Proprioceptive Sense

Movement Sense : Vestibular Sense

Sense of Touch : Tactile Sense

Hearing Sense : Auditory Sense

Eye Movement Skills : Ocular Motor Skills

Using Two Hands Together : Bilateral Coordination

Mouth Coordination : Oral Motor Skills